DATE DUE			
APR 0 5 2011			
MAY 2 0 2011			
SEP 1 3 2011			

EDGE
BOOKS™

ALL
ABOUT
DOGS

LABRADOR RETRIEVERS

By Brekka Hervey Larrew

Consultant: Mary Feazell
Secretary and Judges Education Chair
Labrador Retriever Club, Inc.

Capstone
press®

Mankato, Minnesota

Edge Books are published by Capstone Press,
151 Good Counsel Drive, P.O. Box 669, Mankato, Minnesota 56002.
www.capstonepress.com

Library of Congress Cataloging-in-Publication Data
Larrew, Brekka Hervey.
    Labrador retrievers / by Brekka Hervey Larrew.
    p. cm. — (Edge books. All about dogs.)
    Includes bibliographical references and index.
    ISBN-13: 978-1-4296-1948-6 (hardcover)
    ISBN-10: 1-4296-1948-1 (hardcover)
    1. Labrador retriever — Juvenile literature. I. Title. II. Series.
SF429.L3L37 2009
636.752'7 — dc22   2008001224

Summary: Describes the history, physical features, temperament, and care of
    the Labrador retriever breed.

Editorial Credits
Erika L. Shores, editor; Veronica Bianchini, designer; Marcie Spence and
    Jo Miller, photo researchers

Photo Credits
Alamy/Daniel Dempster Photography, 27
AP Images/Steven Senne, 20
The Bridgeman Art Library/British Museum, London, UK/Thomas Busby, 12–13;
    Royal Pavilion, Libraries & Museums, Brighton & Hove/Richard Ansdell, 11
Capstone Press/Karon Dubke, cover, 1, 6, 7, 10, 14, 19 (bottom), 21, 23, 24, 25, 29
Getty Images Inc./Barbara Peacock, 26; Kurt Hutton/Picture Post, 15
iStockphoto/Tina Rencelj, 18
Photo by Fiona Green, 17
Shutterstock/Fernando Jose Vasconcelos Soares, 5; Joseph Gareri, 28; Kirk Geisler, 19
(top);   Michal Kolosowski, 9

Capstone Press thanks Martha Diedrich, dog trainer, for her assistance
    with this book.

Table of Contents

CHAPTER 1

LOVING LABS

A Labrador retriever races along a pier. A Frisbee whizzes past the dog's head. The Lab leaps gracefully off the pier and snatches it in midair. The dog splashes down into the water and swims to shore. Shaking water from its shiny coat, the Lab returns the Frisbee to its owner. The dog is ready for another leap into the water.

A Favorite Breed

Intelligent, athletic, and friendly, Labrador retrievers are the most popular dogs in the United States. Each year more than 100,000 Labrador retrievers are registered with the American Kennel Club (AKC). Thousands more Labs are kept as pets but are never registered with the AKC.

Labs are suited for many types of activities. A Lab might spend its days playing with kids, hunting, or working. Families love Labs for their loyalty and gentleness. Hunters appreciate their retrieving skills. Police officers and soldiers depend on the Lab's sense of smell.

Labrador retrievers are the most popular dogs in the United States.

5

Lab puppies from responsible breeders are healthy and happy.

Is a Lab Right for You?

Does a friendly, active dog sound like your kind of pet? If so, finding the right Lab can be an adventure. Learning as much as you can about the breed will help make you a better dog owner. A good **breeder** is necessary when buying a puppy. The AKC registers breeders who have the breed's best interest at heart. Some people choose to rescue adult Labs that need homes. These dogs are available through rescue organizations and local animal shelters.

breeder — someone who breeds and raises dogs or other animals

CHAPTER 2

LAB HISTORY

Many people think Labrador retrievers are from Labrador. This area is in the northern part of Newfoundland, Canada. Labrador retrievers are from Newfoundland, but they are not from Labrador. They are from southeastern Newfoundland. St. John's is the oldest city in that region. The Labrador retriever has sometimes been called a St. John's dog.

No one knows for sure how these dogs got to Newfoundland. English and Portuguese fishermen worked in this area as early as the 1500s. The fishermen around St. John's used dogs to help them fish. They needed dogs that could survive the harsh Newfoundland climate and work in the icy waters there.

The fishermen's dogs had to learn quickly and be obedient. The dogs spent long days fetching nets, hauling fishing lines, and retrieving fish that escaped the hooks. The fishermen probably bred their dogs to make them better-suited for these activities. After centuries of breeding, the result was the modern Labrador retriever.

The Newfoundland is a breed closely related to a Lab.

EDGE FACT

In the 1800s, two types of dogs were called Newfoundland dogs. The Lab was called the Lesser Newfoundland because it was the smaller of the two. The other dog, which is still called the Newfoundland, weighs nearly twice as much as a Lab.

Back to Europe

In the 1800s, many English **aristocrats** collected hunting dogs. The Third Earl of Malmesbury noticed Labrador retrievers as they came ashore with Newfoundland fishing boat captains. He began buying and breeding these dogs. The Tenth Earl of Home and the Fifth Duke of Buccleuch also raised Labs. These aristocrats' sons continued the breeding programs. They helped Labs become well known among the wealthy sportsmen in their regions.

EDGE FACT

Today, most Labrador retrievers are descendants of dogs bred by the Third Earl of Malmesbury.

aristocrat — a member of the highest social rank

In the 1800s, many English aristocrats owned hunting dogs.

A Near Wipe-Out

Although the Labrador retriever is popular today, it almost disappeared in the late 1800s. The governments of both England and Newfoundland made rules that caused people to stop breeding and buying Labs.

People in England were terrified of dogs that could spread rabies.

England wanted to keep a deadly disease called rabies out of the country. Dogs infected with rabies can spread the disease. The government feared people might bring rabies into England by buying dogs from other places. To prevent this, they passed the Quarantine Act. People who brought dogs to England had to **kennel** them for the first six months. Rabies could be detected in that amount of time and stopped from spreading.

Kenneling a dog for months was expensive. Selling Labs in England no longer brought Newfoundland ship captains a profit. They stopped bringing the dogs to England.

Meanwhile in Newfoundland, the government wanted people to raise sheep. They hoped this new industry would bring jobs and money to the region. Dogs sometimes killed sheep. The government passed the Sheep Protection Act in 1885. The act taxed people on their dogs. People had to pay a higher tax for female dogs. Many families in Newfoundland killed their female puppies. The population of Labs dwindled.

kennel — to keep a dog in a small fenced area

A Huge Comeback

Thanks only to those Lab-loving aristocrats in England, the Lab survived. In 1905, the Kennel Club in England recognized Labrador retrievers as an official breed. Within a few years, Labs were winning field trials. Today, dogs in these contests track down birds and retrieve them. To win, a dog must follow directions while ignoring distractions.

EDGE FACT

Each year thousands of Labs compete in the 250 AKC-sponsored field trials in the United States.

In the 1920s, wealthy U.S. hunters quickly became Lab fans.

Coming to America

In the 1920s, Labs became popular with wealthy dog lovers in the United States. By the 1940s and 1950s, people everywhere owned Labs as pets. In 1991, Labs beat out cocker spaniels as the country's favorite dog. They have been top dog ever since.

CHAPTER 3

FRIENDLY, HARDWORKING DOGS

What does a Labrador retriever have in common with an otter? Both animals are suited for the water. Their tails are wide at the base and narrow toward the tip. The shape helps them steer in water. Also like an otter, a Lab has two coats of hair. The outer coat is coarse and sheds water. The undercoat is soft and warm.

A Lab's short, dense coat can be one of three colors. Black is the most common color. Other coat colors are yellow and chocolate brown.

A Midsize Dog

A Lab is a medium-sized dog. It stands at least 21 inches (53 centimeters) tall at the shoulders. Muscular and strong, a Lab can weigh 55 to 80 pounds (25 to 36 kilograms).

Labradors' heads are large. They have intelligent, friendly brown eyes and short, hanging ears. Their mouths are strong but their bite is gentle. They can retrieve dead birds with their mouths without damaging them.

Labs have big heads, short, floppy ears, and kind eyes.

17

Social Dogs

Many families choose Labs as pets because of their **temperament**. Labs are social. They like to be with people and other animals. They are not aggressive and rarely bite. Eager to please, they usually follow directions. They even tolerate young children, who might handle dogs roughly.

Labs are active and athletic. They enjoy plenty of exercise. Because they are also intelligent and easy to train, it can be fun to play or work with a Lab. If the weather is cool enough, a Lab can run, hunt, and fetch for hours at a time.

Labs usually get along well with other pets in a household.

temperament — the way an animal usually acts or responds to situations

A Dog for Work

Labs have been bred to learn and obey so they make excellent work dogs. Labs can be trained to find and return the birds their owners have shot. For more than 100 years, hunters have depended on Labs to retrieve ducks, pheasants, and other game birds.

Labs return dead birds to hunters without damaging the bird.

EDGE FACT

People often call dogs that are bred for hunting "gun dogs." Golden retrievers and springer spaniels are also gun dogs.

Labs are used to sniff out drugs in train stations and airports.

A Lab's excellent sense of smell makes it a good detective. Police train Labs to identify the scent of drugs. Labs have sniffed out illegal drugs worth millions of dollars. The military uses dogs trained to find chemicals in bombs. Labs can even find survivors of natural disasters during search and rescue efforts.

At Your Service

Labs lend a helping paw as service dogs. Guide dogs help people who are blind find their way through city streets. Labs can help people who are in wheelchairs by reaching things their owners cannot. Labs fetch items such as the phone, shoes, and the newspaper.

CHAPTER 4

CARING FOR A LAB

Choosing to own a pet is a big investment. Owning a pet involves more than just the cost of buying or adopting it. Dogs need an owner's time and attention. They also need training, food, and veterinary care.

Daily Care

Dogs get hungry for regular meals just like people do. Labs can eat one or two meals a day, but the schedule should be the same every day. A Lab shouldn't snack too much between meals. Too many dog biscuits or other treats can cause a Lab to become overweight. An overweight dog can develop health problems. The amount a Lab should eat depends on the food's quality, the dog's age, and activity level.

Exercise is very important to this active breed. Inactive Labs gain weight easily. Owners should take their Labs on daily walks or jogs. A game of fetch, playtime at a dog park, or other fun activities keep Labs fit and healthy.

Labs need daily walks or jogs with their owners.

All dog breeds need grooming. Labs are easy to groom because their short hair does not tangle. Frequent brushing can reduce how much a Lab sheds. Labs also need their nails trimmed and ears cleaned regularly.

Vet Visits

Yearly trips to a veterinarian keep Labs healthy. Lab puppies should visit a vet for **vaccinations** and to be spayed or neutered. Vaccinations prevent diseases such as rabies. Spaying or neutering are surgeries that keep animals from having offspring. This surgery in turn helps control the population of unwanted pets.

Older Labs need to visit a vet for yearly vaccinations and an exam. Vets check Labs for diseases common in their breed. Hip and elbow dysplasia are lifelong problems for some Labs. The diseases cause crippling pain in the elbow or hip joints.

vaccination — a shot of medicine that protects animals from a disease

Brushing Labs helps reduce shedding.

EDGE FACT

A healthy Labrador retriever can live for more than 12 years.

The command "sit" is an important skill for any dog to learn.

Training a Lab

Lab puppies need to be trained as soon as they are brought home. **Obedience** classes can help owners train their Labs. At these classes, owners learn how to earn a dog's respect and communicate so the dog understands. Dogs learn important commands such as "come," "stay," and "sit."

Proper training is even more important for owners who plan to use their Labs as hunting dogs. Owners begin by teaching their puppy basic retrieving skills. Owners throw a toy for the puppy to bring back to them. As the puppy improves at retrieving, owners can begin to use the real thing — dead birds. Because bird hunting involves Labs swimming in cold water, owners also should help puppies become used to water.

A hunter spends many hours training a Lab to be a hunting dog.

obedience — obeying rules and commands

Labs respond well to positive reinforcement. As the dog learns, owners give rewards such as pats, verbal praise, and treats. A well-trained Lab means both owner and dog know what to expect from each other.

A Loyal Pet

On farms or in cities, at work or at play, Labs enjoy life. They fit in wherever they live. Thousands of people include a Lab as a member of their family. From a pet Labrador retriever, these families receive years of loyal love and enthusiastic affection.

Labrador retrievers are favorite pets to people around the world.

Minooka Junior High School

29

Glossary

aggressive (uh-GREH-siv) — strong and forceful

aristocrat (uh-RIS-tuh-krat) — a member of a group of people thought to be the best in some way, usually based on how much money they have; aristocrats are members of the highest social rank or nobility.

breed (BREED) — a certain kind of animal within an animal group; breed also means to mate and raise a certain kind of animal.

breeder (BREE-duhr) — someone who breeds and raises dogs or other animals

kennel (KEN-uhl) — to keep a dog in a small fenced area

obedience (oh-BEE-dee-uhnss) — obeying rules and commands

quarantine (KWOR-uhn-teen) — the act of keeping something separate from a larger group

rabies (RAY-beez) — a deadly disease that people and animals can get from the bite of an infected animal

temperament (TEM-pur-uh-muhnt) — the combination of a dog's behavior and personality; the way an animal usually acts or responds to situations shows its temperament.

vaccination (vak-suh-NAY-shun) — a shot of medicine that protects animals from a disease

Read More

Bolan, Sandra. *The Labrador Retriever*. Our Best Friends. Pittsburgh: ElDorado Ink, 2008.

Gray, Susan H. *Labradors*. Domestic Dogs. Chanhassen, Minn.: Child's World, 2007.

MacAulay, Kelley, and Bobbie Kalman. *Labrador Retrievers*. Pet Care. New York: Crabtree, 2007.

Internet Sites

FactHound offers a safe, fun way to find Internet sites related to this book. All of the sites on FactHound have been researched by our staff.

Here's how:

1. Visit *www.facthound.com*
2. Choose your grade level.
3. Type in this book ID **1429619481** for age-appropriate sites. You may also browse subjects by clicking on letters, or by clicking on pictures and words.
4. Click on the Fetch It button.

FactHound will fetch the best sites for you!

Index

Minooka Junior High School